Both females (such as the one shown here) and males have **pedipalps**. In mature males the ends look like boxing gloves and help hold on to the female's shell while mating.

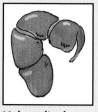

Male pedipalp

The **chelicerae** look like little legs, but they are actually feeding claws.

A horseshoe crab cannot bite. It doesn't even have jaws or teeth! Bristles at the base of the legs knead and push food into the **mouth**.

Book gills, thin sheets of tissue held together like the pages of a book, help the horseshoe crab breathe and swim.

Five pairs of **legs** help the horseshoe crab walk, eat, and dig.

The **operculum** covers the book gills. Eggs and sperm are released from this area.

The **pusher legs** help dig into the sand, push off when swimming, and mold eggs into clusters.

Horseshoe crabs bleed blue **blood**! Copper causes their blood to turn blue when it contacts air; iron turns our blood red.

HIGH TIDE FOR
HORSESHOE CRABS

Lisa Kahn Schnell

Illustrated by
Alan Marks

Charlesbridge

For Marina and Fiora, my own amazing creatures—L. K. S.

To Tessa and Seth—A. M.

Special thanks to the experts who reviewed this book for accuracy: Dr. Carl N. Shuster Jr., Adjunct Professor of Marine Science, the Virginia Institute/School of Marine Science, The College of William & Mary; Gary Kreamer, Aquatic Education Specialist, Delaware Division of Fish and Wildlife, Department of Natural Resources and Environmental Control (DNREC); and Kevin Kalasz, Biodiversity Program Manager for the Species Conservation and Research Program, Delaware Division of Fish and Wildlife, DNREC. Thanks also to Glenn Gauvry and the many others who supported my enthusiasm with their time, knowledge, and generosity. Finally, thank you to Steve Schnell and Alyssa Mito Pusey— this book would not have happened without you.

Published by Charlesbridge
85 Main Street
Watertown, MA 02472
(617) 926-0329
www.charlesbridge.com

Library of Congress Cataloging-in-Publication Data
Schnell, Lisa Kahn, author.
    High tide for horseshoe crabs/Lisa Kahn Schnell; illustrated by Alan Marks.
        pages cm
    ISBN 978-1-58089-604-7 (reinforced for library use)
    ISBN 978-1-60734-785-9 (ebook)
    ISBN 978-1-60734-784-2 (ebook pdf)
1. Limulus polyphemus—Juvenile literature. 2. Animal migration—Juvenile literature.
3. Coastal ecology—Juvenile literature. [1. Horseshoe crabs.]
I. Marks, Alan, 1957– illustrator. II. Title.
QL447.7.S36 2015
595.4'92—dc23   2013049024

Printed in China
(hc) 10 9 8 7 6 5 4 3 2 1

Illustrations done in watercolor and pencil on Fabriano 5 paper
Display type set in Badger Bold by Red Rooster
Text type set in Adobe Jenson Pro
Color separations by KHL Chroma Graphics, Singapore
Printed by Jade Productions in Heyuan, Guangdong, China
Production supervision by Brian G. Walker
Designed by Martha MacLeod Sikkema

It's starting.

One spring night, the first horseshoe crab lunges
onto shore.

They're arriving.

More horseshoe crabs follow. Just as generations have done since before the time of the dinosaurs, adult horseshoe crabs crawl from the muck of their winter homes and swim toward land. Millions of horseshoe crabs head for Delaware Bay. High tides carry them far up onto the beach, where their eggs will develop best.

They're flapping.

On flickering wings, flocks of shorebirds fly through wind and rain, through day and night. Some of these birds weigh only as much as a handful of paper clips. Still, they are powerful enough to fly thousands of miles, from South America all the way up to the Arctic, where they will lay their eggs. One of the few stops they make along the way is on the shores of Delaware Bay.

They're traveling.

Scientists journey to Delaware Bay from around the world. Some come to study the horseshoe crabs. Others come to study the birds. Citizen scientists—both adults and children—come year after year to observe and help the professional scientists gather data. Families on vacation, curious about the commotion, also stop to watch.

They're leaving.

Scientists and vacationers brush sand off their binoculars.
They pack up data sheets, beach chairs, and stories, then
return home to share what they've learned.

They're leaving, too.

Most adult horseshoe crabs ride tides and currents back into deep water. Others won't reach water quickly enough, though, and will die on the shore.

About two weeks later, the young horseshoe crabs burst from their eggs. Now nearly the size of ladybugs, they crawl from the moist sand and swim away to begin their own journey.

It's over . . .

. . . until next year.

A CLOSER LOOK AT WHAT'S HAPPENING

Horseshoe crabs and their ancestors have been on earth for about five hundred million years! For the past ten thousand years or so, they've been crawling onto the shores of Delaware Bay. Despite their name—and all those crab-like legs—horseshoe crabs are not crabs. They are most similar to the now-extinct trilobites. Scorpions, spiders, and ticks are their closest living relatives.

The horseshoe crabs shown in this book are called *Limulus polyphemus* (LIM-yoo-lus pol-ee-FEE-mus). This species is found along the shores of the eastern United States, from Maine to Florida, and also in parts of Mexico. Three other horseshoe crab species live in Japan, India, China, and Indonesia.

In Delaware Bay the greatest number of horseshoe crabs come ashore to spawn in May and June, when the moon is new or full and the tide is at its peak. The male uses a special claw to hold on to the back of the female's shell. As the female digs several inches down into the moist sand, other males gather around the pair. After the female lays a cluster of as many as four thousand eggs, all the males near her release sperm over the eggs to fertilize them. This happens several times a night for four or five nights, until the female has laid between eighty thousand and one hundred thousand eggs.

A horseshoe crab egg develops best in sand that is warmed by the sun and moistened by salt water. The egg also needs oxygen. After about two weeks, or longer if the weather is cool, the horseshoe crab hatches.

High tides sweep the tiny horseshoe crab into the water. It stays close to shore, where it burrows in the sand and eats small invertebrates and bits of plants and dead animals. By the time it's two years old, the horseshoe crab is a little bigger than a dandelion. It moves to deeper water and eats new kinds of food, including algae, dead fish, small clams, worms, and other marine organisms.

Because its hard shell is a fixed size, a horseshoe crab must molt (shed its exoskeleton, the outer structure of its body) as it grows. By the time it is an adult—around eight to ten years old—a horseshoe crab will have molted sixteen to eighteen times and will be ready to come ashore to spawn. A horseshoe crab does not necessarily return to the same beach where it was born. In fact, it may even swim or drift to a different state. A horseshoe crab can live to be twenty years old or more.

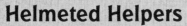

Helmeted Helpers

Horseshoe crabs and their eggs are an important part of the larger food web. Eels and many other kinds of fish gobble up the eggs and immature horseshoe crabs. Sharks and loggerhead turtles eat adult horseshoe crabs. Gulls, raccoons, and other animals sometimes eat horseshoe crabs that have been stranded on the shore. Also, many marine invertebrates live for years attached to the shells and undersides of horseshoe crabs.

Packed with protein and fat, horseshoe crab eggs are the main reason shorebirds, such as red knots, ruddy turnstones, and sanderlings, return year after year to Delaware Bay. To gain weight as quickly as these shorebirds do, a fifty-pound child would have to eat about six and a half fourteen-inch cheese pizzas each day—in addition to normal meals—for two weeks! Although it would be unhealthy for a human, the egg feast helps prepare the birds for their own breeding season.

Horseshoe crabs help humans, too. For centuries Native Americans and other farmers ground up horseshoe crabs to make a (stinky!) fertilizer. Now whelk and eel fishermen bait their traps with horseshoe crabs. Horseshoe crab shells are an important source of a substance called chitin (KYE-tun), which is used to make surgical thread.

Perhaps most important, the biomedical industry uses the blue blood of horseshoe crabs to make LAL, short for Limulus Amoebocyte Lysate (LIM-yoo-lus uh-MEE-buh-site LYE-sate). A simple LAL test ensures that all medicines and medical devices used in our bodies (and those of our pets) are free of harmful bacteria. This includes everything from vaccines and needles to pacemakers and replacement knees. LAL tests also allow astronauts to test spaceships for contamination by microorganisms.

Because horseshoe crabs are so important to humans, birds, and other animals, scientists study them carefully. Spawning surveys allow scientists to detect changes in the number of horseshoe crabs from year to year, while tags placed on the animals help scientists track where horseshoe crabs travel and how long they live. This information enables people to work together to protect horseshoe crab habitats. It also helps determine how many of these animals can safely be harvested for commercial purposes. Although some scientists believe that North American horseshoe crab populations are stable, not everyone is certain. In other parts of the world, horseshoe crabs are endangered.

Up Close and Personal

If you would like to see the frenzy described in this book, you can visit Delaware Bay—the world's center of horseshoe crab spawning—in May or June. On some nights millions of these tank-like animals tumble over one another in the waves and line the shores. You can hardly reach the water without stepping on them. Horseshoe crabs spawn in smaller numbers on numerous other beaches along the East Coast, too. Many scientists who work in these areas welcome volunteers of all ages who would like to participate in spawning surveys.

Although the mass spawnings happen in the spring, you can sometimes see horseshoe crabs in the summer and fall, as well. Wherever and whenever you see horseshoe crabs, if you find one stuck on its back, turn it over so it doesn't dry out in the sun. Grasp the top, rounded edge of the shell—never the tail!—and gently flip the animal over. You'll be holding a fascinating creature with a remarkable history right in your very own hands.

For Further Investigation

Books

Crenson, Victoria. *Horseshoe Crabs and Shorebirds: The Story of a Food Web.* New York: Marshall Cavendish, 2003.

Dunlap, Julie. *Extraordinary Horseshoe Crabs.* Minneapolis, MN: Carolrhoda, 1999.

Hoose, Phillip. *Moonbird: A Year on the Wind with the Great Survivor B95.* New York: Farrar Straus Giroux, 2012.

Horowitz, Ruth. *Crab Moon.* Cambridge, MA: Candlewick, 2000.

Websites

The most comprehensive website for information about horseshoe crabs:
http://horseshoecrab.org/

For more information about shorebirds:
http://www.dnrec.delaware.gov/fw/Shorebirds/Pages/default.aspx

If you see a tagged crab:
http://www.fws.gov/crabtag/

To participate in spawning surveys:
http://www.dnrec.delaware.gov/coastal/DNERR/Pages
/DNERRHSCSpawningSurvey.aspx

Activities

Visit the DuPont Nature Center at Mispillion Harbor Reserve, Delaware:
http://www.dupontnaturecenter.org/
Visit the Nature Center of Cape May in Cape May, New Jersey:
http://www.njaudubon.org/SectionCenters/SectionNCCM/Introduction.aspx
The annual horseshoe crab poetry, writing, and art contest is open to all grade levels, pre-K–12:
http://www.horseshoecrab.org/act/contest.html

Videos

Washington Post video about counting horseshoe crabs in Delaware Bay:
http://www.youtube.com/watch?v=VpJ3qX0Mwy8
PBS video about horseshoe crabs:
http://www.pbslearningmedia.org/resource/bf10.sci.lv.ls.fossil/the-living-fossil/
A short, informative video about horseshoe crabs and their relationships with red knots and humans:
http://thekidshouldseethis.com/post/52136681072

Selected Bibliography

"Green Eggs and Sand." Thank You Delaware Bay website.
http://tydb.mobiusnm.com/general-green-eggs-and-sand
"The Horseshoe Crab: Natural History, Anatomy, Conservation, and Current Research." Ecological Research & Development Group website. http://horseshoecrab.org/
Shuster, Carl N. Jr., Robert B. Barlow, and H. Jane Brockmann, eds. *The American Horseshoe Crab.* Cambridge, MA: Harvard University Press, 2004.
Tanacredi, John T., ed. *Limulus in the Limelight: A Species 350 Million Years in the Making and in Peril?* New York: Kluwer Academic/Plenum, 2001.
Tanacredi, John T., Mark L. Botton, and David R. Smith, eds. *Biology and Conservation of Horseshoe Crabs.* New York: Springer, 2009.

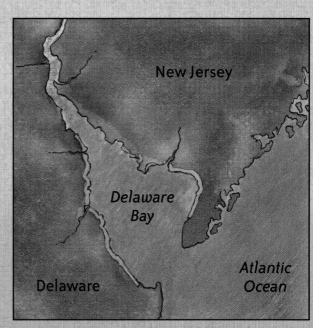

= Prime spawning area

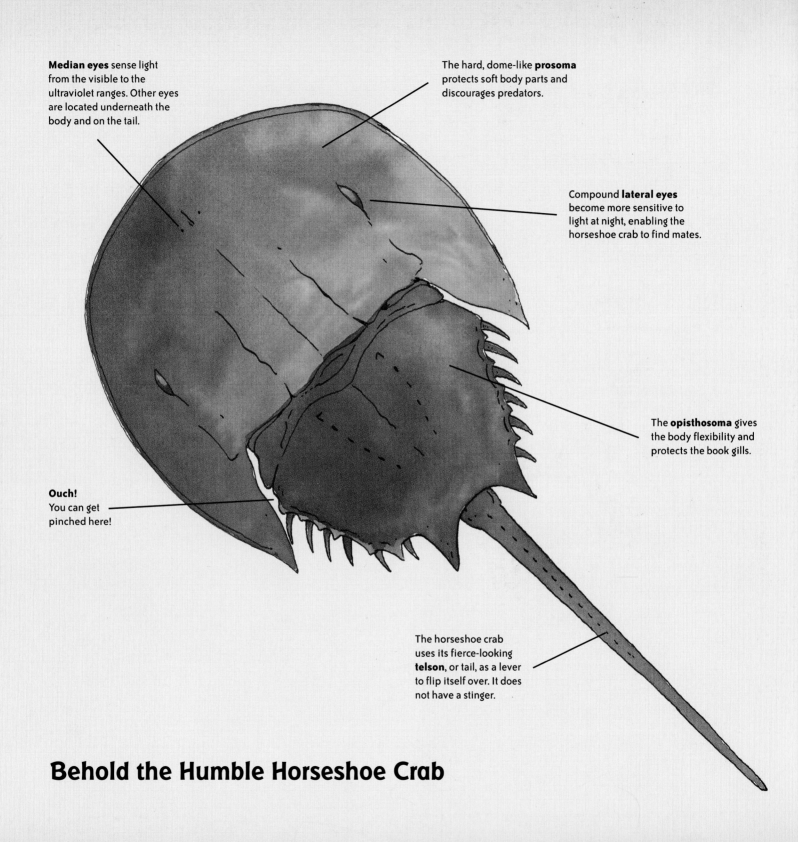

Median eyes sense light from the visible to the ultraviolet ranges. Other eyes are located underneath the body and on the tail.

The hard, dome-like **prosoma** protects soft body parts and discourages predators.

Compound **lateral eyes** become more sensitive to light at night, enabling the horseshoe crab to find mates.

The **opisthosoma** gives the body flexibility and protects the book gills.

Ouch!
You can get pinched here!

The horseshoe crab uses its fierce-looking **telson**, or tail, as a lever to flip itself over. It does not have a stinger.

Behold the Humble Horseshoe Crab